IN KIND

IN KIND

POEMS

by Maggie Queeney

University of Iowa Press Iowa City

University of Iowa Press, Iowa City 52242
Copyright © 2023 by Maggie Queeney
uipress.uiowa.edu
Printed in the United States of America

Cover design by Susan Zucker
Text design and typesetting by Omega Clay

Printed on acid-free paper

Library of Congress Cataloging-in-Publication Data
Names: Queeney, Maggie, 1982– author.
Title: In Kind: Poems / Maggie Queeney.
Description: Iowa City: University of Iowa Press, [2023] | Series: Iowa
    Poetry Prize
Identifiers: LCCN 2022041393 (print) | LCCN 2022041394 (ebook) | ISBN
    9781609388973 (paperback; acid-free paper) | ISBN 9781609388980
    (ebook)
Subjects: LCGFT: Poetry.
Classification: LCC PS3617.U446 I5 2023 (print) | LCC PS3617.U446
    (ebook)
    | DDC 811/.6—dc23/eng/20220928
LC record available at https://lccn.loc.gov/2022041393
LC ebook record available at https://lccn.loc.gov/2022041394

Cover art: *Pleasures Known*, 2019 (detail), by Kathleen Ryan.
Materials: agate, amazonite, amethyst, aragonite, aventurine, black silk
stone, bone, calcite, carnelian, chalcedony, Ching Hai jade (dolomite and
fuchsite), chrysanthemum stone, citrine, crystal quartz, feldspar, fluorite,
freshwater pearls, garnet, hematite, jasper, labradorite, lepidolite,
magnesite, malachite, marble, moss agate, onyx, quartz, rhodochrosite,
rhodonite, rhyolite, rose quartz, rutilated quartz, serpentine, smoky
quartz, tektite, tiger eye, tree agate, turquoise, unakite, yellow turquoise,
ruby in zoisite, acrylic, glass, steel and stainless steel pins, polystyrene,
wood and steel tools, fishing rods, steel trailer, and rubber tires.
Size: 174 x 91 x 79 inches.

For Monica Berlin, in memory always

My intention is to tell of bodies changed
To different forms . . .

—Metamorphoses, 1.1–2

In the most severe cases, the victim retains the dehumanized
identity of a captive who has been reduced to the level of elemental
survival: the robot, animal, or vegetable.

While the majority of . . . patients complained, "I am now a
different person," the most severely harmed stated simply,
"I am not a person."

—Dr. Judith Herman, Trauma and Recovery

The trees are not trees, anyway.

—Cynthia Cruz

Contents

I They did not know, in the darkness, in what fashion
The change had come upon them; they were lifted
On no great mass of plumage, only on wings
So frail you could see through them.

—*Metamorphoses*, IV.408–411

The Female Liver

Here hunters eat the heart
from the kill before a careful
choreographed gut and drain.
There's time before the vein

will cauterize and the body seals.
So I oil my eyes for the room,
to stutter past the hooking
detail. I need more nets

of my own. More teeth cast
in steel and to be thinner—more
streamlined bone, less joint.

I need the poison I scraped,
saved, the rest of the body
rendered all holster.

My Given Name

Here I am, telling myself the story
Of myself again. The mammal of me,
Lowing my lone note,

Grit both the middle and the start of it:

A bit of sand or shell shard, the hard
Speck of stone or flint or bone or beak—
What cannot be broken back

Into nothing, but offers an ever
Smaller division: this is what made me
What I am: *Mar*—as in mark, as in wound,

As in sea. As the root word *pearl* at the center
Of me: damage and flaw. I freak iridescent,
Cultured or wild. My pet forms: Magpie,

Then Maggot. Magnificent, imprisoned dirt
Magnified to trapdoor, magnet of hurt,
My sputtering beauty. Bowing to the ground,

I listen to the rush inside my body, hush of gas
Blooms of blue petals ringing the jet, as nerves
Singing their leviathans' sibilant songs deep

In the ocean of me. I ward and seal and cover.
I swallow. I round into a swelling nacre
Moon, the only gemstone bred out of a living

Creature. Or the woman reborn whole, limbs
Spilling out of the dragon's belly, the scales,
Meat and fat parted and heavy as the velvet

Curtains framing the spotlight, the beam
Of hot gold gracing the tramp of me. The rough
Labor of me, my midwife. My insane, my orphaned,

My born homeless. I spiral my shelter, my own

Shell of bone. My reptile mother formed over
My body a bell that gleams and refuses to ring:
Tongued into a stone shard licked harmless,

Hearted in an arrowhead fitted to a pin.
The skin grown through the armor.
The fur grown over the scar of the collar.

Font

We had Qs tattooed to our wrists, exploding
the letter to measure ourselves a new font
against our matching tangle of veins.

Distortion we knew, was inevitable—the wrist
a hinge in almost constant use.

The Q an eyed letter, its descending lick
immediate as the optical nerve
to the brain, the bright ponytails
we wore as children. They made
our heads into hearts, arteried into the wider
system of trees, the street of families
other than ours that fed and bedded us.

When our mother wanted to kill
and couldn't, she utilized the inanimate,
the unable to scream: a car over a foot,
boot into wall, our bedrooms
rebuilt on the lawn in the careful

framework to a fire. We started to speak
in abstraction—how *glyph* slides
into *nymph*, we burrowed a tunnel
to the dumb, the animal. The mythological

where no one ever turns into a girl.
Always a girl into flame, into bird,
into rock. And our mother in smoke,
her skin a web of vents, in the dark
of her new house slanting south
of a lake. The Q here a noose, a snare
waiting for a triggering foot,

an eyespot we plotted to confuse
our own traitor hands, shaped in her shape,
a seed shooting into any ready break.

6

Metamorphosis: The Daughters of Minyas Deny Ecstasy, Transform into Bats

As sisters, we knew the color of blood. We knew the interior afternoon dusks
we worked our looms through. That what occupies the hand occupies the mind.

We knew women danced in skins outside town, grape vines linked into crowns
ringing their skulls. The faint panting their palms struck

from drums filled our rooms the way a mouth fills a lung.
Each dug her feet into her own fatted shadow, into the stamped dank ground,

in anklets of mulch and musk and the sharp reek
of something we knew not to name.

Our hands kept rooted inside our looms. Our hands kept crawling
the warp and woof and we tied our tongues with stories

of lovers, the heavy-lidded forest, the toothy trunks,
and furred ground. The dark middling a fruit. The bell in a cup.

We knew to trust nothing by touch. Trust not the work the sun does,
not even the weaving as it starts to green, shoot, and root the tiles.

We sang ourselves new bodies
the volume of our old hearts.

We sang our chests into fists, our blood
into the wine revving our new forms forward.

Gorgoneia

Days, I make myself hungry, nights
I am ensnared in hair, knotted locks,

that *charm* is drawn from incantation,
and most people who are killed are killed

by people they know. I am caught in the ruined
body of my mother, the bit that pulled her lips

back into a grin, the invisible knee that urged her
into mirrors, into the reflective faces

of infants and men. I am caught in what she took
for love. That incantation breaks words

back into sound, sound into song, a shield
that presses the bearer down.

I am caught in the eye, a wounding wound
that recites, the subtraction beauty radiates:

a halo, the rotting root of a tooth,
a black hole bending light.

Alterations

At thirteen, our thin bodies bent,
flattening skirts and dresses over the floor.
Our teeth held pins between tinted lips,
forcing us to indicate what we wanted to say
with our arms as if leading a prayer
over the sequins and suede, the embroidered
flowers and birds we had dissected
back into flat approximations, part
by part, of our size and shape.

We centered the bloom of paper patterns
unfolded and creased, road maps
to the ghosts of trees, to shadow bodies
listing and whispering against the floorboards
in the house drafts, the indifferent air
that moved when we moved.

We held our scissors pointed away,
as if their slender blades could pull
a truth north out of the room
where we bent,
mouths streaming thread.

Exhibit

The hawk clutches a piebald hare, planks of wing
strung at the apex phase of its flap, a chevron
leading the eye back to the transfixed, dusty hide
in-claw, to the nest strewn and waiting in down

and bones and fledglings. Parent and prey
sway, strung in constant arrival, a violin
waxing. The eye practices each stitch
binding the skins over strata of wool

as if running scales, plays along
the rippled, room-temperature pelt.
Shellacked branches grow
in stalled lightning to edge the tableau:

what is left of the hands
that shaped and sealed and chose.

What Color You Would Be If You Could Be Any Color

If a sin, then my greed for materials things,
my envy of others. If of the earth, then groan
and whisper, and I swallow the sun. I am
difficult to obtain, untamable, and everywhere

wild and tangled. Marked in stalk, wrapped
in a ribbon about youth, I spread in a rooted flood
and break rock with parched strands of hair.
I have killed whole families at home, the women

paid to shape me into flowers and the women
who paid to pin the flowers to their breasts,
drag yards in a bloom or plume from their waists.
Centuries of men have labored to make me behave

unbraided, unmixed, pure of woad and weld,
fine and exile. I am the mother never known.
The middle child, feeding us all from her own
faded bruises, cloud ceiling in tornado season.

Strain in Horror Vacui

I too abhor the vacuum,
the pulling empty

empty of empty, lunar inhalation, the heft
of the portraits of the dead

slivered inter-page
I too shore up against

the flooded, fractured, besieged,
and the fruit to rot soft and sweetly

on the counter, dresses hung
in beheaded, female strata

of impossible plumage
in the closet, the flash and clang

of jewelry crude as handmade
lures and the constant unspooling

of music from the corner of the room
while the television mutters aquarium blue

across the wall windowed in pictures
I too break

silence against that, I crack
jokes, prod a laugh, mock, affect

as a bird fakes flightlessness
in a circular hobble, weaves and drags

a wing in one half
of a cape and danger

away from the breast of the nest
that offers, platter-like, the defenseless eggs—

rhyme an upended bottle, *medicine*
and *poison*, the cut

of meat that disappears with a sweep
of an ink-black top hat

from the waxing white plate
ringed in chipped wild flowers

vased wild flowers performing
their death in a softening technicolor

while tablecloth patterns path
back and away and when I pray

I pray to the tic stitching moment
into future, utter into mimic,

into distract, into hide, and I cry out
in the melodic strains of my prey

Scar Wear Song

An animal licks the red wound into white scar,
forcing her saliva into salve, old flesh into new.
I step back into her old dress, worn as I wear,

to return to were, I sound the graft, the soft bark
where we are: the cut the scion covers, seals to use.
An animal licks the red wound into white scar.

My past self traces, triangulates: my here to her far.
I tell her to kill it. My mouth a mirror we lean into
then through—this sweat, her dress, the ever I wear.

I weigh my live against her dead. Even in the dark
a body keeps a red deep inside the vein's coursed blue.
An animal licks the red wound into white scar.

I recite what happened, again, a spell to disappear
the lariat question's buzz: why didn't, what did you do.
In this dress, an old rag of the shape the body wears,

I line my eyes with black, my lips red as a skin's tear,
all to summon the outline of our other future: you.
An animal licks the red wound into white scar.
I walk into her dress of never, ever worn as I wear.

Glamour

The look I am hunting: the one
that through color and cut glares

the starer into a skull or a skein
of lightning, a switch

stalled at dawn, or the gloaming
along an equator. What fascinates

I shine like flame-blackened foil,
a rhinestone snoring at lake bottom,

a wreck's brass-bound astrolabe,
bright as hard tender, newly minted,

mewling and naked under
oil-slick pleather sieving light,

prism-like, my limbs sing their siren
song, pull ribbons of pure note over

the pack's snarl and bark, teeth pop,
dangling chain of saliva snaps—

deep under, I stay
seamless as a safe, a rust-sealed letter

box, corroded pill case, my insides
scoured to looking glass

by a tangle of wind trapped,
a cyclone circling the space

the size a doll's eye makes,
panting my small breath.

Ex Ovo Omnia

In the waiting room, a photograph
on the magazine-tiled table: the skeletal remains
of a bird, delicate as needles, curled
over speckled rock. The beaked skull
scissored an angle of air, wing bones parted
in a pantomime of flight
where stubborn feathers still clung.
The obscene, bleach-white ribs
like an unhinged bracelet encircled
the pellets of plastic that had starved
the bursting animal dead.

After, instead of the grayscale
ultrasound, alien as Jupiter's striated shell,
the nurse at my side had searched, eyes pulled
edge to edge as if she were scanning a passage
for a seed-sized heart in contraction,

I remembered the heart-sized body rotting
in a blast pattern of feathers and bone
tracing tongue-want and stomach-need,
ardor and immolation—venom's root
is love. A bearable hunger begins.

II

Her body dries and shrivels till voice only
And bones remain, and then she is voice only
For the bones are turned to stone.

—*Metamorphoses*, III.399–401

Salvage

A winter spent sifting the secondhand hanging
racks of moth-gnawed wool, zippers
snarled along dress spines, unraveling hems
where thorns of old sweat prick, traces of blush

rose the collars. Balled receipts bloom
faded sums, smoke ghosts, and perfumes'
foreign tongues coil like hibernating snakes
inside purse linings. Tine scores mar

the faces of plates and time-tarnished links
of chain scribble a box's scarred velvet
insides—what draws me, sweat-enmeshed,
bolt-enshrouded, naked inside the infinite

other shes, to mock, try to disguise, to hide
the old hag following in her floor-length fur
like a mass grave held open and shining
a rayed aureole out of the wings of shot

silk lining to her bare, her milk-blue
skin scribbled maroon, pubic hair dull
as a pelt salted and taut, hanging
to cure over the headboard of a bed.

The Liver and Lust

When others want, I leave them
the bone, the slabs of gristle.
They have their own flesh,
their own tongues wetting

the charred meat in their teeth.
Outside, I strike rock with rock.
I strike the liquid hearts locked,
hunt the next from the ground

to weigh my hands, to occupy
these fingers and arms, where
one ends and another starts:

my palms bark, knots rose
over the vital parts to mark
what beats, what invites.

A Charm, A Series of Survivals

After, I salved the wound of it. Buried the rape in silence.
Words: a ward away. Bound, binding: the moth-like silence.

My grandfather's calf rotted saccharine, unseen under a throw.
Summer, my mother yelled, "Outside!" In the winter, "Silence!"

The wolf came clad in the skin of the prey's kin—my friend
waited until I could not say no. He wrote his yes into my silence.

My father told me his comfort, that I knew how to live poor.
I hoard a heap of gold specie between my thighs, silent.

Each wailing infant, wild cat ululating to his prey calls me
by my first name, the last speaker of my language: silence.

Deception in Animals (Camouflage)

discipline, a craft   a deep study, how to be   what wants

to kill me   I make my reduction   of shadow, cryptic

behavior   I match the background   take what is not

wanted for my own   inedible, transparent   body, I remember

other colors, other   disruptions, the break and   blur of outline

rock resemblance, bark resemblance, resemblance   of silver, of water

I take light and turn   light, turn shape   into shape, into bleed

into over, into   my echo out   turn echo into   my own

echo, all call   into echo, my own   reverberations, spreading

Love-wildered/Re-wilding

To return, still and embrace
the collapse and scrape, the break,
burn and stall—offer the body

as alms, as bait, steaming meal
centering the plate—the shape
described in negative space—

the shining arrow of ether
skewers breast to air, mouth
in a shaft of sunlight—skin knits

into the harness of leather, collar
fitted to youth, bark rings
over the rusting nail and lace rots

in a drawer's dark casket, close
as silent prayer—the damage
inflicted to stay

damage salves and balms—
generations of finches shot
out of air, acres of trees burst

into light and fume, banks of down-
soft ash along the forest floor
skinned like a scalp

must—abandon alone proves
never enough—speak
through that tether, the tongue,

a lash with two ends, a door
dividing bed from the night
not known and the dark

of the brain—wildernesses
beyond name—to be left
untouched or taken away—

After-Assault Counting Out

That shirt. That night. I wore
that skirt, that dress, those tights.
Those heels I wore. I drank
those drinks: one, two, three—

My birthday, that night: thirty-three.
That morning, the first, I found
the bruise. I looked, that morning,
I found my shoes.

I found my shirt. That skirt found me.
I wore that night. That night wore me.
I looked, that night—drank one, two,
three: that shirt, that dress, those jeans,

those heels. I looked. I wore that
bruise that now wears me.

Metamorphosis: Punished, Echo Disappears, Repeats the Last

what woman has not told a story and been punished
                              for the story, the telling, I stared

into, then through, like a moon, my own undeserving
                              desire, soothing the moss-furred

rocks at pool bottom, I punish lost hunters, fling
                              their last frantic syllables back

careless as fingernail clippings, laughter, shed hair
                              sharp as glitter, I mimic and mock

flirt with acting the savior to any stranger, calling
                              the caller deeper into orbit

the gravitational heart, the heavy white shrouded
                              summit, I freeze, I starve the ones

who laughed at my burning body, choke each
                              name in my own relentless mirror

I carry a body-long shield, a bloom beyond
                              touch after I fed my sorrow my

sorry body, strip of bloodless flesh by strip
                              to float in the cold socket of a cave

no one chooses the shape their immortality takes
                              outside the body, abandoned glove

the blush, the scatter of bones I left, now numb
                              as stone as the air vibrating bow

string, I am waiting to be called by name, found
                              in any other mouth, I went to look

into his mystery, into the water, the dark blank
                              unbroken, there is no lakebed, no

stars here anymore, no more throat waiting
                              to sound my voice in his language

Cry Wolf

What difference between crying and calling,
cursing and summoning, the frantic limbs
of a lamb and the bared legs of a child.

What difference between the desire to laugh
at the adults running, spades and rakes in hand,
and the need to know they would run at the call.

Remember most do not know the name
of what they want, even as they are wanting—
the body incandesces, numb and ecstatic,
as it is destroyed.

Remember the wolf, drawn only
by gut and jaws, insistent as divining rods—
heart rearing at her name called,
finally, between the trees.

Metamorphoses: The Female Into

laurel tree, limbs bent and twined into crown   heifer   bank of marsh reeds,
handful lashed into pipes, song in another breath   a clutch of conifers, weeping

amber   black bear, quarry, constellation   white crow, black crow   grass-
cropping mare   flames   voice repeating the last   darkened mulberry

fragrant incense seeping out of the ground   violet-like flower tracing
the sun's path rock   darkness-seeking bats   sea goddess   rock

rock   rock   rock   rock   seabirds   serpent   a prize, a bride
monster crowned in snakes, ossifier, weapon   black and white magpies

arguing in near-language   water-flowing-fountain   half-alive, half-dead
flock of tuneful, maiden-faced birds   one of a pair of mountains   crane

stork   ash-gray spider weaving her traps in the corners of the ceiling
corpse   corpse   corpse   corpse   corpse   corpse   corpse

spring weeping into the summit's anorexic air   nightingale   swallow   traitor,
mother, cast-off ex-wife, witch, weaver of the poisoned robe, deadly gift,

filicide, unnatural   marble figure   corpse   patricide, exile, heron   diadem
in the sky   guinea hens   five isles   a further island   linden tree

slave then fisherman then mare then bird then cow then deer   weasel   lotus
that bleeds when plucked   lotus   spring flowing from a shrub oak

male   twice-dead shade   rock   whores, shame burning their bodies red into
rock   myrrh   lioness   grove of oaks   halcyon   male   barking

bitch snapping her jaws   snow-white doves   deadly whirlpool virgin-
faced hounds snarling between her thighs   water, then nothing   a statue

of a woman   a star inside her husband constellation   corpse, living female,
fountain of chilled water

Glamour

....

After, I sought out only cover. I shied from
Color, from structure, from cut. I denied

The body's actual size, assumed the coats
Of men, several times larger and stronger,

To be able to slouch, to scrape my blackening
Feet over the floorboards, shake the hard music

Out of chain anklets, thick hoops and bangle
Bracelets. My only magic was sympathetic:

I pressed my body into whatever wild hide
I could find—shield of leather, fur, sheltering

Roof of layered wool, and turned animal—
The thick silk a spider hides her eggs

Inside—that was me. Darkening my lids
Larger, coloring eye after eye neon-bright

At my hair's part, to descend my sides
In a second skin. I repeated. Light and shade

Alternate a body to walk into—glitter and shine
Saved for the parts farthest from the heart.

Ubi Sunt: A Look Book as Primer

You can have anything you want in life if you dress for it. —Edith Head
You know, if you don't want to entice a rapist, don't wear high heels so you can't run from him.
If you're wearing something that says, "Come and fuck me," you'd better be good on your feet.
—Chrissie Hynde

A-line, as in the roof of a body, as shelter, as cover

Black lace-edged, the bra strap half-buried, dusty inside with roadside gravel

Cuts, she assesses as if before the butcher counter, shapes the body is worn into

Dresses hang in the unlit closet, empty and wire-shouldered, light as kites

Embroidered letters initial the back of the collar, a small heart mends a moth hole

Fur edging and she returns to the animal, bristling, each strand banded as a canyon

Glove lost and hung from the picket, waves or warns, commands *stop*, wards away

Hair she wants and does not want—what complains to the brush, bleeds at the root

I count the girls, the women I knew almost murdered by men who loved them

Jacket pulling the arms from her chest, the stitches spread, gape, I separate

Knits and the pattern I have learned my whole life repeats, changes, returns

Leather boots tough as roof shingles, belt a whip-thin equator, her butter-soft wallet

Made by hand or made by machines that were made by hand or made by machines

Newness a shine she surrounds herself with, a vehicle to climb into

O: the shape of a face, sound of her beauty and error, how terror flares an eye open

Pilled wool pulled from her sweater, shed into a path of bright and tangled seeds

Quilted: air and space hold her own body's heat, fabric and feather: a net, a trap

Ribbon reddening the grass, serpentine to the forked end, the silks furred in dirt

Slip hung from the curtain rod, darker at the ends, dripping even after wrung

Tights: soft dark casings to hide the legs and the skin of the legs, cradle and bind

Under the others, the thinnest of things designed to cover, to flare, bare, and flutter

Velvet, the pile of pet, plush of mushrooms or mold, she grows softer

Worn until worn, then worn-out: the fleeting life span, she mourns the purchase

X where she last was, the only stitch she knows to mend with

Yoke she threads her head through, worked in flowers, in glue jewels, the weight of

Zero: how much longer the body lasts, the new fabric wrapped in sheets of plastic

The Dress Dreams of Hands

All I ever wanted was to be stilled
as a mare is stilled

by the weight of a body across
her spine, shiver of fingers

in a waterfall shines her flank
smooth as the familiar waist

hanging in the closet. To be split
open to my innermost

self and not find another body
beating silent and perfect and

alien as laughter as my seams left
groan and my skirt swells

in a wind still sweetened
with distant grasses, crushed

and fragrant. I cover and wear,
cut and enhance. I cower inside

the heavy amber air of the basement
bar, under the words of a man

near stranger, each tender as
a hoof feeling out the field

in the dark, describing a love
long gone with more kindness

than I have ever accepted or allowed,
near breaking into flames

from flinty shame, taut between fear
and want, the cringing electric

haunches and starving heart
of a stray.

III

One flew to the woods, the other to the roof-top,
And even so the red marks of the murder
Stayed on their breasts; the feathers were blood-colored.

—*Metamorphoses*, VI.671–673

Dead Reckoning

Once I had been able to ask for things.
Then I started to search the ground
the way nesting animals hunt
spills of paper, fistfuls of hair snarled
and hopeless from lasting too long.

I followed the aching planes that formed the corners.
I traced the negative space in winter-bared trees,
the hole formed out of my chest and waist and arm,
the rooms of the houses I still walked in the dark.

Trackers cut circles to find signs
of passing, disturbed earth,
and so I wound the ground
into a bouquet of figure eights,
trying to locate a print, a hollow,
a bent stem or snapped branch
to testify to all that happened,
what triggers this constant
curve back into the curve
of an eye, the shape
a child takes
inside the mother.

I found a hand, a mouth, a spool of intestine.
I found my legs make and remake snakes,
fangs clasp at hoops of spine.

The Liver as Regenerator

....

I trace the story read off a scar.
Beams striking horizon bend
and return the world, line
by color. The liver returns.

The sky-blackened vulture spirals—
I return to recite and lick the red,
the pearl-white knitting skin.
I return to recite what I cannot afford

to do: this organ the closest thing
to living I can carry.
I guard this dark distiller,

this filter part. A rough foot
from the heart, it waits
to be called, quartered, handed out.

In Kind

The window washers' scaffolding ropes rap against the window glass, against
my blurred portrait cast back through my pupils' black

to the office thirty-three floors above the street. The lake waits in a distant,
disoriented curtain. Beyond, my sister's body hangs

like a tongue from the basement's ceiling of pipes, throat striated a daybreak
in negative. The kitchen floor is still scribbled in her broken limbs, crushed skull.

Her scarlet bath stains the porcelain as she rises to sitting, laughs, lifts a shaft
of wheat-gold hair over a bony shoulder, splatters the tile in a beadwork of blood.

She paces the mean length of the hardwood hallways, rattles snaps of thin silver
chain and moans her own name through the doors. Gust at the head of the stairs,

my own form watching my sleeping body, thin infant's cry in the basement, rose
blooming in a locked trunk, she draws my life out in an endless scarf, a soft leash,

each step I take away. She follows, cradled head smearing the dark arterial blood
into her hip; stares but does not look, worn into static symbol by her rough stagger,

measured as land breaks water into waves, the heaving body of a bitch in heat.
Black hole of hunger, quicksand's unending need, she hunts the next. My eyes,

divided between the hands at my sides, each so close in kind to the hand that draws
knife blades into her hips, wrists. Untrusting, unknowable as strays, they bathe,

arrange and paint the life-like face, then bury, burn each, one by one. Nothing and
no one ever enough.

House
....

Some form floorboards,
others a bed. Everyone left
is wall. They indicate windows.

We talk the occupants
into being and bend our limbs
from where they stand.

One board, the shriek
of a child. Another, the thump
of the one walking towards her.

The rest are silent, watching
the pushes of air in the room.
The window frames twitch.

The bed, not needed,
crawls through the walls
to clap its jaws

at the crows clutching
their nails into ground
outside, impatient.

Specie

I knew about the gun. And the gun, it knew about me.
The money was gone. We were surrounded by things.

Days were spent in subtraction: ghost-like ends of bread,
eaten oranges, eaten eggs. The heat circulated the vents
and made our bodies lighter. Furniture cast shadows
over the floorboards, pathing the bedroom to bath,
kitchen to front door to window and back.
Days we spent dusting, wet cloths in our hands.

Days we spent keeping the moving parts noiseless
with grease. We kept casings from dust, engines
from rust, shed rags like rosary beads ringing
our feet. We kept windows locked, blinds turned
against the soundless, churning street,
the light exhausting color out of text and cloth.

The gun hung mute and heavy inside the drawer
farthest from the door. At night, claw marks scored

a radiation around the lock gleaming a gold, distant
sun, small enough to hide with a hand.

Last Case on the Murder Task Force

A telephone splices the night—lit nerve ending
or lightning strike—and the child rises all lung, all mouth

and howl. The man rises from inside the mother, rises
from the casts of his fingers clutched into the sheets

and separates the boy's head from his chest.
He runs, knife in hand, body in arms, floor to floor,

beating on doors as the thin limbs jog at his sides.
He palms the boy's head, guides the jaw back

to the neck, but blood leaks and blacks
his bared chest in the stills taken later that night.

The state assigns my father to the defense. He twists
the tinny, stripped facts into a cast outlining a life.

He tells the jury the man grew up a thing burnt
by his grandfather, his mother, that his thin body smoked

and scabbed taut. And then the foster homes and the beatings
and the drugs and the howl and the boy and the knife.

The state threads a new heart into the man's chest.
He is kept living. He is sentenced to death. Nights on trial,

my father walks the floor with my infant brother, crouped up
and wailing the mucus out of his lungs, his mouth with a howl.

My mother sleeps, buried tight as a drawered knife,
gleaming through what beauty her children had left.

Metamorphosis: Procne Serves Her Husband a Meal of His Own Child;
Changed into a Swallow, She Nests in the Palace's Eaves, Does Not Weep

The elder, I always did what was expected: bent a path
through the world like long grass with my body paved
a way out of our father's kingdom's perimeter birthed

a male heir within the year inside the funereal torch-lit
bed, under the planetary gaze of an owl scoring a count
of talons of the days left into the fragrant headboard

and, more, I beseeched, I asked for what I needed, then
believed when *he*, face lowered, delivered the news
of her death at sea, the waves' swallowing her body.

I shed the saffron robes. I bore the black, voluminous
and liquid as smoke or a squid's cloud of ink. *He* was still
hidden to me. And dear Philomela. How often, as sisters,

were we placed side-by-side, praised for our identical
brows, identical size, oneness sounded where we two-ed:
two eyes, two arms ending in two hands boned

like two wings, two legs swelling into our plural
hips holding a galaxy of jelly-like eggs, any of which
would split and split and split until a man emerged,

capable of this: keeping a girl-child alive, blood
still dried brown on her thighs and her tongue
cut out so every bite that she eats, breath breathes,

her wound wounds. Shut up deep in the forest,
a hind butchered cut-by-cut, she is kept fresh, alive.
How could I not kill and salt my own son, half

his, after what had been done, and boil and season
and serve and only after tell him what he eats.
Do not blame the knife for the cold of the blade.

Do not blame the reflection of the face *he* made.
Unnatural breeds unnatural; strange breeds
strange. The shit and the dirt floor and dark stain

her split maidenhead made. Trained by her needle
into the longest and last instance of *his* name, I do not
call, hidden in the thick stampede of branches

high in the tree, or the one who it is said was half-
me, but changed as I was changed, feathered
and beaked, still voiceless, now another species

who hears, lifted by the long muscle of air swelling
the roofless sky, sky without wall, without lock and door
and key. The horizon in the black of the eye, her without me.

Deception in Animals (Mimesis)

I want to scare my shoulder line, a bluff of blown-out hair, fine

and brittle as spun sugar, antennae my bracelets clack an alarm

shine dazzles, bands of color spread like water breaking the rock

of another puzzle of neon, markings I have never felt

alone, save lonesome so many eyes constellate woods, skies, I

draw each black buttery pupil a hissing droplet of ink

my beloved recitations, beloved repeat, what I can afford

to lose and live, my distant destroyer circles, sounds out

my language traces, the pattern repeats, the pattern reds

Glamour

My thirteenth summer, I was not at home. My mother
Threw away every piece of clothing I owned. I returned

To the closet emptied bare as a breastbone, the whine
And rattle of the empty dresser drawers, sudden

As an infant. I stood inside the air of another woman's
Inhalation, still and damp. Years after, the only

Path I could strike was *more*: bricks of skirt rustled
Into turret. I wound bolts of cloth into bandage or soft

Cast or cocoon or habit. I collected dresses many sizes
Larger, dreamed of all the bodies crowded into those

Forms. I strung charms into the wristfuls of chime
I move through. My reverse bloom, I drew and tightened,

Grew seamless and unmarred, the scarred parts sealed.
She told me my need means I would have to return too—

Generations of gazelle bow their slim velvet snouts
To the same opaque crocodile-laced waters, to the clouds,

Light as the roving fleece drawn into fine, strong threads
By the spindle. Inside the billows of rough habits

Of holy women, seers were born whole to brick cells
Slight as their own lost limbs, a spill of matchsticks

On the stone floors. A high window the area of an open
Book to allow a beam of light. A tunnel of gold, streamer

Of air, faint sound, and nothing more.

Auspice

The robin flew at the window
for days, seeking entrance
against the seamless pane,
wingtips like two clutches
of dry paintbrushes. The twig-thin,
twig-strong claws combed glass
as wings and breast sounded
an insistent knocking
we listened to in every room
except the basement
where my sister slept
in a drug-heavy sleep.

My father drew the blinds, taped
gilded wrapping paper over the pane,
but the fist-sized chest, furrowed
in seams of deeper, dull red,
beat out a refrain in the days
we waited and traced
the possibilities that branched
out of the dark knot inside
her left breast.

The robin would not stop
its brute attempts at egress,
kept thrusting its frantic chest
at the glass as if pressing
the rusted badge of the males
of its species into a slide,
a plate to be read. My father,
when he spoke of it, always
said *she*. He spoke always to,
but never of me.

We Moved Houses

Another born and we moved houses.
The house was packed into boxes.

Our hair darkened. Boxes stood empty,
dark in the crawlspace below the floor.

We grew inches of arm and leg.
We packed boxes. We moved houses.

We slept behind locked doors,
in our beds inside our rooms like boxes.

We traced the heights of strange children
penciled into kitchen doors. We called

the numbers laddering hallway walls.
Our teeth pried out. Our teeth grew in.

We packed boxes. We moved houses.
We composed maps to dead bodies

and treasure, left ransom letters in drawers.
Our father struck down interior walls,

prised open the floors. The house
was put into boxes. We packed.

We moved. We learned not to love
the shapes certain branches bore.

What Kind of Animal You Would Be If You Could Be Any Animal

I was born ungrateful, hungry and haunting:
a scavenger. Omnivorous, I nose the sides
of highways, the arrangement of other women's
hair, shining yards of tinsel torn from a float.

I look long into the buttery face of the infants
howling in register lines and search for my own—
a cabbage head sweating fuchsia, the dress that
keeps the shapes of the last owner, what I fold

myself into: a fur collar coated in another
century's cigarette smoke, paper bag wadded
into a greasy hive housing burger rinds, tacky
strands of cola beading a cup. I have my tastes,

but I would take, finally, anything. There is no end
to the hunt, or wanting. Even my dreams are veined
in twists of wire, tatters of fiberglass sheeting.
A bouquet of squeaking, bright and bitter weeds.

IV

She still kept spinning; the spider has not forgotten
The arts she used to practice.

—*Metamorphoses*, VI.146–147

Metamorphosis: Prosperina, Queen of the Underworld, Proclaims into the Thaw

Not so unlike the stars: the bone-bright
electric messages through the weaving
I mimic the language of seeds:
a door, when scored, or the soft
What travels through the hungers
without leaving: a cathedral of stalactites
of an underground lake, the tip
pierces its reflection, doubles into
vertebrates, seamless as a woman
into rope. All grows toward what it knows
then binds. There is no change without
bend, without consequence,
of a flower, golden-throated, haloed
above a spill of green. Now, bound
thinks to ask what cracks open, unfurls
inside my body—the half-dead
any other part before. I am the hybrid
who remembers and the one who
thaw, the hibernating and the hunger
the dream of a mother who does not
like to die. The one where I do not have

rootlets of trees hum
that traps dirt into my ceiling.
my hide, hull, what splits, like
dissolve of groundwater pores.
of others. There is no return
cleaves the mirror-still surface
of minerals in suspension
a column, the bilateral radiation of
chewing the ends of her hair
to need: a vine climbs,
repeat—how many times did I
to gather beauty to me in the form
inside a bone-white starburst
by what I was said to eat, no one
roots into or through the dark
half of me cared for more than
plait of two strands—the one
does not remember, freeze and
that drives me to back into
have to ask what it feel
to ask which death. Which time.

The Anthropomantic Liver

It's the shake, the trembled after-night
that thrums the body into one long nerve.
It's the heat peaking, the spires
recording distant, unfelt earthquakes.

Blood surges the vein, pulls in time
to distant tides inside the body
offered, pinned ground to side, dark
part of the eye wound up to the sky,

exposing the egg-white to the flickering
length of the knife. Flint strikes the flame
to feed the divine the invisible

in pitch-hued fumes ascending
from the nest knit in bone black—
what remains, returning to earth.

The Nature of the Idea-Horse

The idea arrives in the form of a horse,
long jaw drawn between the curtains belling
a blue parenthesis. Her head turns the room
in silhouette, in the dark eye that reflects

the walls in full sail and distends the floor,
the tangle of furniture, the pale and strange
human form. Sun strikes her spine
into a horizon line and alien spices rise

from her hide to perfume the room.
I offer apples halved into hearts, palms of sugar.
I offer my fingers as bits, arms as reins. To break,
to be broken, I surrender my legs. My pulse takes

her flexing back's gait as together we cast
on the rushing current of grass
a creature in negative,
double-headed, of one mind.

At the Museum of Natural History

stalled foxes stare to the visitor's left
as if startled by their own long-ago deaths
breaking out of the trees and the wolf lowers
a dark-gummed snout to the featureless white
bottoming the case below its bone-slim forelegs.

Across the hall, pigeons and doves unfurl
wings graduating into flight. Owls clutch
and cower on abbreviated limbs, staring
for a dart, a flash of hide while hummingbirds hang,
a series of iridescent commas, from pegs.

Each composition depends like a door opening
into a receding, remembered world
where the salvaged bodies occupy
assigned spaces, uninterrupted for decades,
ringed in gleaming leaves and recycled air,

thrumming scraps of abandoned web in the corners.
Out the hall window, flocks migrate, distant-dark
against approaching night, day waxing
the invisible, shielding sphere and we forget
our name: merciful predator, singular prey.

Glamour

A corruption of grammar—what knowledge
I have come by comes through the eyes

To my hands—lightning runs the skeleton:
Skull to spine and phalange, dirt, then grass.

I gather what else can be cast: die, a spell,
A glance, lots, off—the lace edge that frets,

Frays, when caught. I keen at the bellow, then
Burn the thick marrow. Mar the smear of kohl

Into a plume of smoke above the burn line:
Hearth-eyes. Left alone too long, my long bones

Curdle into shatter. The gloss works my lips
Into lather. I train a tongue to slaver

At the word *meat*. I cannot say how this means:
Invisible weaving, a safety net turned sideways

Into snare. The stocking's run pulls the eye
Elsewhere—*warn*, then *worn*, then *wear*. I trace

The shape to know. I keep *want* from *want*.
Silver of hammers, silver of scales. Then gold.

Victim: Root

Even in the Latin, female. I trace
my mother's mother's mother's

name, letters splayed like legs
or branches, the bones I had been

scolded, *grow*, that I had read
burned white in sacrifice.

Told what it was to be holy, as a child
I applied the dustiest rose lipstick

my mother owned, chewed the bud
made under the veil stained my cheeks'

color, a slight bride in a sheer slip
before the origin that rendered me

conquered, as *victor* clanged a few entries
further. Each imitation pearl glowed

like knowing against the knots of hair
torn smooth. The floorboards groaned

over my head. I was trained to hold still
under a man's hands, that virtue lies

in the lines of the hind, sleek ankle stuck
in the air as she struck still to hide.

Then with a darkened blushing bit of rag,
I worked it off after: the female hand

that arranged; the unlocking bedroom doors
lining the hall like a deck of cards, a puzzle

of blank backs: the chance of the draw, the pull
of the heavy curtain; the dark audience,

their rehearsed gasp marking the night
from evening, the white shock of glove

quick as a dove darting over the tornado-
shaped gold light ending in a halo, a hem

to circle a single stocking foot, sleek heel.
I too designed to fashion another body

after my body. To press that other smaller
version forward into service, the place

I was made to take, impossible to identify
in the dark, the daughters I will never have

and never know among all the bodies
that made my body then made my body

not my own.

The Women

more than the men, even. The ones who looked
like I looked. Who called my name in a voice
I could not identify from my own on recordings.

The women who wore my cheekbones, who when
they wanted to shake their younger, stupider selves,
saw my smaller body, always X years behind. X sizes

smaller. X less. When solved for, I was the variable
named *accident*. The second sister, the child ticcing
through the countdown of an explosive device,

echoing down the oceanic tiles of the school hall.
I was the engine of the chainsaw stalling. The ghost
who splintered the cupboards, who buried the silver

eel of the knife into the floor. I covered the rooms
in a seamless cloud of flour, opened the front door
to the night as we slept. There was no word

in the languages I knew for the species of help
I needed, so I dug a hole and buried the house
keys in the garden, fed necklaces into the hollows

of trees. I was the one who knocked from inside
the ceiling, who chewed the garlands
of red and blue plastic behind the walls

down to each wire spine. I was the silent fire
detector, the dead batteries chirping like a toy bird.
The one who is never named. When summoned,

        I shattered the lamps, cracked the glass covering
           the faces inside the picture frames.

        To repeat is to make strange, make what happened
           smaller, farther away. It was the women

who laughed, who asked what else I thought
would happen. The women who told me they knew
what I would do. That I had to come back.

The women inside the fascia and bone I lived in, who
doubled, then multiplied, copied my features over and over
the landscape until even a thick blanket of snow

was the milk-blue pale of the skin that shielded us all
in false innocence. How the red rose over years. An infant
will be drawn to an adult with large eyes,

the proportions of another newborn. I remember
the faded blue, frantic darting like a bird wrapped in the soft brine
of ocean air, caught in the red netting of my grandmother's eyes.

That morning on the staircase when I was, I think, five.
She clutched a tumbler of orange juice, cried that he needed
sugar. It is strange, what children will remember

and not remember. Did I look, then, from behind
my mother's thigh. Did she need to see him bluing, his thick
stillness in the rental house bed, too. What is the difference

between the remembered and the imagined, between
wanting and action. I remember how long it took to name, to own
the thick bulb of joy pressing against my breastbone,

the tender thirsting rootlets, the invisible tendrils
that fractured and strangled, suckled the bright blood out of
the women I come from, and then broke into bloom.

Deception in Animals (Thanatosis)

half a lifetime spent   playing at it   as if trying on another's

dress   to see myself   as her, death always

another woman, flicking her hair   into flame   the trick is not

to try to not move   the hand away   from the heat

but to kill the hand   how long do I spend still   and rigid or still and

yielding to the repulse   of what wants me   what   I want—

to empty   the body, to want   the body   empty of want, I

feign death, make apparent   the empty body   white as

that stare of   unblinking, far sky   when do I   become

My Rough Labor

ends again in the hard child I was,
breech-birthed, chin caught on the crag

of my own pelvic bone. I learned
to kick away, like the earth, to return,
like the earth, warmer under my feet

than the shadow dragging at the side of me
in a strange, dim tongue licking the vinyl

siding of others' homes, lapping the momentary gold

spilling out a lit window, where other forms
moved inside the frame, and covered me in a coat.

I learned that pain will force the body open
until the body forces the body closed.

I learned to widen from the snake of my spine,
to flood and double into a strand, a timeline
of inkblots fanned into the patterns I hold between

my hands when I need to see into me: the ouroboros
formed of centuries of bodies inside my body.

I learned from the species that devour their own,
the reborn, and those who kill to live: the snake,
the spider, the corvid, and me, mouthing

mute into *mutable*. I took the shapes
of what I ate, rid the old body inside a shudder,

worn thin as a clutch of ribs holding
the heart like some slender, caged treasure.

I learned to measure with the pain scale
tacked to the exam room wall. I learned from the burr

digging its many hooks into a mare's rough coat,
and the thousand futures seeded
between the identical heads of flowering weeds

of the meadow I stared into until I could
no longer see. I repeated
the ghost of me, night after night, until changed. This

is the way I escaped. I learned to speak as the magpie
mocks a human voice. I learned that my eyes
could be twin beams boring tunnels, sweeping

a scythe through the long, gold grass,
held by the same rough hands I wrap around my new

milk-blue heels kicking free of me. I slapped
the first breath into my own back, then fattened
at my own chapped breasts.

It is human, this plummet
into pattern. Human, the faces that stare
back out of the rock, the rough maze of bark

wrapping the trunk, plumages of wild birds at perch.
Spill of stars. Grain of the carved wood
headboard. Electrical outlet. The house

staring down the empty street. A crowd of many
species of bloom. A shed bedroom.

A child, drawn into the arms of her mother,
inside the path of her natural predator.

I did not burn into an ash fine as silk.

I did not quiet my own wild cries.

Deep in the middle of me, others wait,
each smaller, more perfect than the last,
eyes seamless as pearl earrings.

Inside each yolk, the soft bones of her hands and feet
appear identical to the skeletal starts of fins or wings.

Identical, the thousand galaxies of gemmy eggs,
my many burning earths, my bodies left, skins shed.

I learned to multiply, cradled inside
my divide. I learned we all swell into the familiar

pattern of the abandoned seashell,
ring swallowing, holding ring.

Born again into the breach, the hard child I had
and was, begins again to end our rough labor.

Raised

I clawed a way out of the hard soil
Packed in the impressed spade

Backs, a naked hole filled long
As a body, to air, to rise blood-

Sequined, dirt-streaked, dirt kohling
Each eye, mouth of dirt embroidered

In splinters of coffin wood, knuckles
Gleaming ruby with my own welling

Blood that tapers in nails edged
In the crescents of moon I used

To drag my body out. Years after
My father bequeathed me

My true nature: accident
Of my mother, who later revealed

The body as trap. I snap closed,
Seamless as mud or molten silver,

Each finger parted from the palm
Throwing handfuls of dirt light as

Confetti, fragrant as the arrangements
Of flowers offered only to yellow

Then scatter their nail-shaped petals
That whisper like *daughter*,

Trace like armor the soft form
Beating blood under so long after

The mourners return home, return
The good dark clothes to the hanger.

My Hand

She has always made her own way, looping loose
Stitches into horizon after horizon of tangled
Brambles. She bites red patterns, embroiders lariats
With thorns, extends her baited snares. What I do

To remember what I need to remember—slow my arm
To stall my mind and mute the memory the muscle
Still holds. Trained by the narrow chutes of red links,
Blue rules, I now stagger through the unbounded field

Of unbroken white and refuse to admit or own
My own danger. Even lost and bleating my location.
My stitch and limp unspooling a graphite trail across
The toothy white paper that leads, always, back

To me, what I know: I hide and hold in equal measure.
What could not be held against me after.

Metamorphosis: Arachne, Struck Silent, Radiates Silk

Born into the house of a small god
                         of color, of pounded
weeds, boiled blooms, ground roots,
beetles light as gossamer, as shells disintegrate

into ferrous sulfate dunes, like Dawn I unfurled
worlds, threaded vivarii, bound limbs,
the chest and eyes of the figures and forms cast

in a net equitensed in the loom frame
true as a door opening, and yes, I allowed
praise to raise my skill akin to the gods', I swelled

like thirsty fleece steeped
in purple-black vats of tint.   Wonderwork, they called
the fingers drawing string into cloud-like masses of silk

and wool,   and light building
from my hands smooth as if dyed and I
demand to know why the divine appears

in crone-form, not found
inside the girl born mortal, but enters
her locked cell in a shaft of sun, takes

the momentary shape of a bull,   the beating wings
of a swan, tunnel of gold light,   flame, and serpent.
The reluctant lovers, the ravished, captive, left to live,

bear those beaks and feathers, hides and scales, hooves,
antlers, snouts, tails.   Beauty always
the transgression, silence   the punishment.

Mouth-shorn, ear-shorn, nose-shorn,   I wonder
now at that sad trap of house-whitened limbs
that hypnotized nymphs—   these new legs, needle-

thin multiply stitches four-fold, turn the invisible
unbreakable   trick the wind
into servant   driving meat and meal

as I wait, Queen-like, ash-fragile and fanged,
spinning above the shining crowns of hair bent
to the looms in the old house   my new room

ACKNOWLEDGMENTS ....

Thank you to the editors, readers, and staff of the following publications who first gave these poems, sometimes in radically different forms, homes: *Account* ("Metamorphosis: Punished, Echo Disappears, Repeats the Last"; "Metamorphosis: Prosperina, Queen of the Underworld, Proclaims into the Thaw"), *American Poetry Review* ("Glamour," appears in Part I. in this collection), *Colorado Review* ("What Kind of Animal You Would Be If You Could Be Any Animal"), *Crab Orchard Review* ("Metamorphosis: Arachne, Struck Silent, Radiates Silk"), *Entropy* ("Auspice"), *Fugue* ("The Dress Dreams of Hands"), *Guernica* ("The Women"), *Handsome* ("Metamorphosis: The Daughters of Minyas Deny Ecstasy, Transform into Bats"), *La Vague Journal* ("The Anthropomantic Liver"; "The Liver as Regenerator"), *Los Angeles Review* ("My Given Name"), *Matter* ("Ex Ovo Omnia"), *Meridian* ("House"), *Nashville Review* ("Metamorphosis: Procne Serves Her Husband a Meal of His Own Child; Changed into a Swallow, She Nests in the Palace's Eaves, Does Not Weep"; "Metamorphoses: The Female Into"), *Nimrod* ("Font"), *North American Review* ("At the Museum of Natural History"), *Painted Bride Quarterly* ("Cry Wolf"; "Last Case on the Murder Task Force"), *Pinwheel* ("Specie"; "Strain in Horror Vacui"), *Packingtown Review* ("Alterations"; "Gorgoneia"), *Prelude* ("Exhibit"), *Seneca Review* ("Victim: Root"), *A Shadow Map: An Anthology by Survivors of Sexual Assault* ("After-Assault Counting Out"; "Salvage"), *Slowdown* ("Metamorphoses: The Female Into"), *Southern Poetry Review* ("We Moved Houses"), *Southeast Review* ("The Nature of the Idea-Horse"), *Southwest Review* ("Scar Wear Song"), *Split Lip Magazine* ("Dead Reckoning"), *Third Coast* ("On the Female Liver"; "On the Liver and Lust"), and *TYPO* ("Love-wildered/Re-wilding"), and *underbelly* ("In Kind").

I want to thank everyone who has read and written in community with me, especially Holly Amos, Mairead Case, Kate Garklavs-Saul, Dolly Lemke, Amy Lipman, and Patrick Samuel; the community at Syracuse University; and the participants of the Forms & Features workshop series, who continue to expand my understanding of what poetry can be and do.

My many teachers, thank you: Michael Burkhard, Dympna Callaghan, Arthur Flowers, Mary Gaitskill, Amy Hempel, and Bruce Smith. My first poetry teacher and teacher poet, Monica Berlin, who expanded the world we live in, thank you. Brenda Fineberg, who connected me to *Metamorphoses* and other monstrous women, thank you. Christopher Kennedy, who saw me, thank you. Mary Karr, who saw who I could become, thank you.

"Alterations" is for Christine De Cavarlho, who first showed me how to be an artist, how we could remake the world around us. Thank you.

Bridget Lowe, thank you for helping me to learn to be in the world, and for your belief in my work. Learning with and from you and your work is one of the major gifts of this life.

Katherine Litwin, this book would not exist as this book without you. Thank you for connecting me with the books I needed to write these poems.

Brenda Shaughnessy, thank you for seeing this manuscript as a book, and for believing in my work. My many thanks to everyone at the University of Iowa Press for their labor and care, particularly Ann Przyzycki DeVita, James McCoy, Susan Hill Newton, and Margaret Yapp.

My gratitude to my birth family, my father, my brother, my three sisters, my two nieces, and my chosen family. You know who you are.

This book is for Alex.

The lines of *Metamorphoses* quoted in this book are Rolfe Humphries's translation, published in 1969 by Indiana University Press, the first translation of this poem I owned.

"Ubi Sunt: A Look Book as Primer" was inspired by "Abracadabra, an Abecedarian" by Karenne Wood.

"House" was written after the poems in Vasko Popa's *Games* series.

"Metamorphosis: Arachne, Struck Silent, Radiates Silk" was inspired by Rebecca Solnit's reimagining of the Arachne myth.

Iowa Poetry Prize
and Edwin Ford Piper Poetry Award Winners ....

1987
Elton Glaser, *Tropical Depressions*
Michael Pettit, *Cardinal Points*

1988
Bill Knott, *Outremer*
Mary Ruefle, *The Adamant*

1989
Conrad Hilberry, *Sorting the Smoke*
Terese Svoboda, *Laughing Africa*

1990
Philip Dacey, *Night Shift at the Crucifix Factory*
Lynda Hull, *Star Ledger*

1991
Greg Pape, *Sunflower Facing the Sun*
Walter Pavlich, *Running near the End of the World*

1992
Lola Haskins, *Hunger*
Katherine Soniat, *A Shared Life*

1993
Tom Andrews, *The Hemophiliac's Motorcycle*
Michael Heffernan, *Love's Answer*
John Wood, *In Primary Light*

1994
James McKean, *Tree of Heaven*
Bin Ramke, *Massacre of the Innocents*
Ed Roberson, *Voices Cast Out to Talk Us In*

1995
Ralph Burns, *Swamp Candles*
Maureen Seaton, *Furious Cooking*

1996
Pamela Alexander, *Inland*
Gary Gildner, *The Bunker in the Parsley Fields*
John Wood, *The Gates of the Elect Kingdom*

1997
Brendan Galvin, *Hotel Malabar*
Leslie Ullman, *Slow Work through Sand*

1998
Kathleen Peirce, *The Oval Hour*
Bin Ramke, *Wake*
Cole Swensen, *Try*

1999
Larissa Szporluk, *Isolato*
Liz Waldner, *A Point Is That Which Has No Part*

2000
Mary Leader, *The Penultimate Suitor*

2001
Joanna Goodman, *Trace of One*
Karen Volkman, *Spar*

2002
Lesle Lewis, *Small Boat*
Peter Jay Shippy, *Thieves' Latin*

2003
Michele Glazer, *Aggregate of Disturbances*
Dainis Hazners, *(some of) The Adventures of Carlyle, My Imaginary Friend*

2004
Megan Johnson, *The Waiting*
Susan Wheeler, *Ledger*

2005
Emily Rosko, *Raw Goods Inventory*
Joshua Marie Wilkinson, *Lug Your Careless Body out of the Careful Dusk*

2006
Elizabeth Hughey, *Sunday Houses the Sunday House*
Sarah Vap, *American Spikenard*

2008
Andrew Michael Roberts, *something has to happen next*
Zach Savich, *Full Catastrophe Living*

2009
Samuel Amadon, *Like a Sea*
Molly Brodak, *A Little Middle of the Night*

2010
Julie Hanson, *Unbeknownst*
L. S. Klatt, *Cloud of Ink*

2011
Joseph Campana, *Natural Selections*
Kerri Webster, *Grand & Arsenal*

2012
Stephanie Pippin, *The Messenger*

2013
Eric Linsker, *La Far*
Alexandria Peary, *Control Bird Alt Delete*

2014
JoEllen Kwiatek, *Study for Necessity*

2015
John Blair, *Playful Song Called Beautiful*
Lindsay Tigue, *System of Ghosts*

2016
Adam Giannelli, *Tremulous Hinge*
Timothy Daniel Welch, *Odd Bloom Seen from Space*

2017
Alicia Mountain, *High Ground Coward*
Lisa Wells, *The Fix*

2018
Cassie Donish, *The Year of the Femme*
Rob Schlegel, *In the Tree Where the Double Sex Sleeps*

2019
William Fargason, *Love Song to the Demon-Possessed Pigs of Gadara*
Jennifer Habel, *The Book of Jane*

2020
Emily Pittinos, *The Last Unkillable Thing*
Felicia Zamora, *I Always Carry My Bones*

2021
Emily Pérez, *What Flies Want*

2022
Melissa Crowe, *Lo*
Maggie Queeney, *In Kind*